BRAW BRAW BR
STUFF TU
FAE FAE
SCOTLAND OTLA

RAW BRAW BRAW
UFF STUFF STUFF
E FAE FAE
AND SCOTLAND SCOTLAND

BRAW BRAW BR
STUFF STUFF STU
FAE FAE FAE
SCOTLAND SCOTLAND SCOTLA

RAW BRAW BRAW
UFF STUFF STUFF
E FAE FAE
AND SCOTLAND SCOTLAND

BRAW
STUFF
FAE
SCOTLAND

BRAW
STUFF
FAE
SCOTLAND

BRAW
STUFF
FAE
SCOTLAND

BRAW
STUFF
FAE
SCOTLAND

BRAW
STUFF
FAE
SCOTLAND

BRAW
STUFF
FAE
SCOTLAND

BRAW
STUFF
FAE
SCOTLAND

BRAW
STUFF
FAE
SCOTLAND

BRAW
STUFF
FAE
SCOTLAND

BRAW
STUFF
FAE
SCOTLAND

BRAW
STUFF
FAE
SCOTLAND

BRAW
STUFF
FAE
SCOTLAND

BRAW
STUFF
FAE
SCOTLAND

BRAW STUFF FAE SCOTLAND

Copyright © Rhodawn Ltd trading as Bookspeed, 2012

Compiled by Kingsley Dawson.

All rights reserved.

Published by **doodlemacdoodle** in association with Summersdale Publishers Ltd.

Bookspeed, 16 Salamander Yards, Edinburgh EH6 7DD
Tel: 0131 467 8100
Fax: 0131 467 8008
sales@bookspeed.com
www.bookspeed.com/doodle

Printed and bound in the Czech Republic

ISBN: 978-1-908661-01-2

Disclaimer
Every effort has been made to provide accurate information in this collection. Should there be any omissions or errors in this respect we apologise and shall be pleased to rectify these in any future edition.

BRAW
STUFF

FAE

SCOTLAND

doodlemacdoodle

INTRODUCTION

doodlemacdoodle is very pleased to bring to you *Braw Stuff from Scotland*, a fascinating collection of Scottish people, ideas and discoveries from Neolithic times to the modern day.

Dipping into this book will inspire and amuse you, making you proud of your connection with Scotland whatever it is!

I hope this little book will tempt you to follow a path, real or virtual, and discover even more about this amazing country.

Kingsley Dawson
St Boswells
January 2012

Braw Stuff fae Scotland is the third book in the 'Dynamic Words from Scotland' series and you can find details of our first two books at the end of this book.

£100,000 bank note

Sir William Forbes of Callendar, a self-made millionaire, coppersmith and landowner, was born in Aberdeen in 1756 and astounded contemporaries when he purchased the estates of Linlithgow and Callendar by auction with this specially printed bank note. The estates had been confiscated from the Jacobite Earl of Linlithgow after the 1715 rebellion.

Adhesive postage stamp

Claimed to have been first proposed by
James Chalmers of Montrose in 1838.

Arbroath Toasties

Smoked haddock, egg and cheese,
cooked together, with added black
pepper and piled onto toast.

Artificial diamonds

James Ballantyne Hannay, from Glasgow, believed that he had synthesised diamond in 1880. However tests decades later established that he had not done so, although the processes that he developed were useful in the subsequent production of synthetic diamonds using technologies not available at the time.

ATM (cash machine)

Inventor James Goodfellow, born in Paisley in 1937, is generally accredited with the creation of the modern Automated Teller Machines (ATM); cash dispensers accessed using his patented Personal Identification Number (PIN) system.

'Auld Lang Syne'

Should auld acquaintance be forgot,
And never brought to mind?
Should auld acquaintance be forgot,
And auld lang syne!
Chorus: For auld lang syne, my dear,
For auld lang syne.
We'll tak a cup o' kindness yet,
For auld lang syne.

Rabbie Burns

Australian national anthem

Peter Dodds McCormick emigrated to Australia in 1855 and composed the words and music of 'Advance Australia Fair'. First performed in public on St Andrew's Day in 1878, it rapidly gained popularity and was sung by 10,000 people at the inauguration of the Commonwealth of Australia in 1901. It replaced 'God Save the Queen' as the national anthem in 1984.

Aye, right

Is it only in Scotland where two positives
make a negative?

Bank of England

This amazing idea was proposed by
William Paterson from Dumfriesshire
in 1691.

BBC

The oldest and largest broadcasting company in the world had as its first Director General, Stonehaven-born John Reith. He was committed to impartiality and to 'inform, educate and entertain'. He stood up to the government in the General Strike of 1926, broadcasting impartial information to the whole country.

Ben Nevis

At 1,344 m, this is the highest mountain in Britain and is climbed by close to 100,000 visitors annually. Most take the Pony Track built in 1883 to take visitors to the Observatory at the summit which also opened in that year. The Observatory was continually staffed until 1904, when it was closed due to inadequate government funding!

Gordon Bennett

Who was he? Well, it seems there were two of them: a Scottish father and son who were both involved with *The New York Herald.*

James Miranda Berry

Celebrated doctor and army surgeon who graduated in Edinburgh in 1812 and became Inspector General of Hospitals. This notorious dandy and flirt (who had fought a duel over a woman) was discovered to be a woman herself after 'his' death.

The bicycle

Not only is Scottish blacksmith Kirkpatrick MacMillan thought to be the inventor of the modern bicycle, but he was also involved in the first recorded road traffic offence when he knocked over a pedestrian in the Gorbals.

Birlinn

Type of boat used especially in the Hebrides and West Highlands of Scotland in the Middle Ages, and is a version of the Norse longship. Also the name of the celebrated Scottish publisher established in 1992 by Hugh Andrew.

Birth control

Edinburgh-born Marie Stopes wrote and published her two controversial books in 1918: firstly *Married Love*, concerning feminism and marriage, and then *Wise Parenthood*, about contraception. These works and her subsequent opening of Family Planning Clinics created a great deal of indignation and opposition from all major churches, which objected to her demolition of the myths and taboos surrounding female sexual pleasure, health and fertility.

Bovril

John Lawson Johnston of Roslin came from a butchering family and emigrated to Canada in 1871. While there he developed Johnston's Fluid Beef which became known as Bovril and was supplied along with other meat products to the French Army for which he was awarded the Order of the French Red Cross.

Brahan Seer

Known in Gaelic as Coinneach Odhar, the Brahan Seer worked for the third Earl of Seaforth in the middle of the seventeenth century. He predicted the building of the Caledonian Canal, the Piper Alpha disaster and the affair that his employer was having in Paris – for which he was sacked.

Brent Crude

This oily trading benchmark was named after the Brent goose by Shell which developed the Brent Oilfield to the north east of Shetland in 1971. It was Scotland's oil?

Buick Motor Company

David Dunbar Buick, born in Arbroath in 1854, emigrated with his family to America two years later. He subsequently settled in Detroit and founded the Buick Motor Company in 1903 which passed out of his ownership three years later, and was ultimately owned by General Motors. Thirty-five million cars have been produced which carry his name.

The Butt of Lewis

The Guinness Book of Records claims
this is the windiest place in the UK.
There is only open ocean between here
and North America and the Arctic Circle.

Calcutta Cup

The first ever Rugby International was played in Edinburgh (in Raeburn Place) between Scotland and England in 1871 – Scotland won by one goal and a try, to one try. The scoring system was different at that time.

Caledonian Canal

Designed by Thomas Telford and William Jessop, the Caledonian Canal includes the massive eight-lock flight at Banavie, known as Neptune's Staircase.

Castlemilk Moorit

A rare breed of domestic sheep
originating in Dumfriesshire; bred in the
1900s from an original flock of
ten ewes and two rams.

Chicken Bonnie
Prince Charlie

Fried chicken breasts with added
Drambuie; said to have been served
to members of the MacKinnon clan in
gratitude for their help after the
Battle of Culloden.

Chilean Navy

Lord Thomas Cochrane, originally from Culross, became one of the most celebrated practitioners of coastal warfare in the early nineteenth century. In addition to distinguished service in the Royal Navy, he also assisted the rebel navies of Brazil, Greece and Chile in their independence periods.

Cleits

Over 1,400 cleits have been found all round the islands that make up St Kilda. These small drystone structures, with open sides and covered by slabs of earth, allowed the free flow of air and were used to store foodstuffs and fuel.

Clootie wells

Are places of pilgrimage in areas with Celtic connections. Magical wells, once common, were places where 'cloots' or pieces of clothing of the sick were taken and suspended from nearby trees in the belief that as the cloth fades, so too will the illness. The tradition lingers on, and one of the most celebrated sites is on the A832 on the Black Isle, featured in Ian Rankin's novel *The Naming of the Dead*.

Cloud Chamber

C. T. R. Wilson from Glencorse,
Midlothian worked in the observatory
on the summit of Ben Nevis during
1893. He made observations of cloud
formation which he subsequently aimed
to reproduce on a smaller scale in his
Cambridge laboratory by expanding
humid air within a sealed container. For
his invention of the Cloud Chamber he
received the Nobel Prize for Physics
in 1927.

Comet paddle steamer

Designed by Henry Bell from Torphichen, the *Comet* was the first steam-powered craft to offer passenger journeys anywhere in the world – and this doon the River Clyde in 1812!

Billy Connolly's banana boots

Now on display in the People's Palace in Glasgow.

Crabs

Eaten in Scotland since the Mesolithic Era and before agriculture was established; archaeologists have retrieved crab remains from sieved midden material near Applecross in Wester Ross.

Curling

Invented in medieval Scotland, an old
curling stone inscribed '1511' has been
found in a pond in Dunblane.

Decimal point

John Napier (see **Logarithms and Napier's Bones**) introduced the decimal point into common usage.

'D.I.V.O.R.C.E.'

Billy Connolly's comedic version of the
Tammy Wynette song became a number
one hit in 1975 when he sang it on
Top of The Pops.

Douglas fir

Named after David Douglas from Perthshire, the celebrated botanist and explorer born in Scone. In his short life, before dying in mysterious circumstances in Hawaii in 1834 at the age of thirty-five, he introduced over 240 species of tree, shrub, flower and herb to the UK.

Ecclefechan tart

Fabulous shortcrust pastry piled up
with dried mixed fruit and nuts – from
Ecclefechan in Dumfries and Galloway.
Best eaten in the Café Ariete in Moffat,
warm with their own ice cream.

Edinburgh Duck

Also known as Salter's Duck, this is a device that converts wave power into electricity. Invented in 1974 by Stephen Salter as part of a research programme influenced by the 'oil shock' of the early seventies, it was a result of his studies of a lavatory cistern at Edinburgh University. A prototype was installed on Loch Ness in 1976, but funding for the project declined during the oil glut of the 1980s. It has been reinstated in recent years.

Edinburgh Zoo penguins

Brought to us by Edward Salvesen from Antarctica in whaling boats from the Christian Salvesen Leith-based fleet in 1913.

Eighteenth-century Bank Wars

The Bank of Scotland was established by an Act of Parliament in 1695, and was subsequently suspected of Jacobite sympathies. The Royal Bank of Scotland, its oldest rival, was set up by charter in 1727 and the following 25 years saw a period of savage competition, the infamous 'Bank Wars', when each bank tried to drive the other out of business. A foretaste of things to come 250 years later!

Electric Brae

An optical illusion on the A719 near Dunure in Ayshire creates the impression that a car can be drawn uphill by some mysterious force. A regular visitor during the Second World War was General Dwight D. Eisenhower who had an apartment in nearby Culzean Castle. Beware of slow moving vehicles!

Encyclopaedia Britannica

First published in three volumes in
Edinburgh between 1768 and 1771.

End to End

John O'Groats to Land's End (JOGLE)
or Land's End to John O'Groats (LEJOG)
is a popular journey with cyclists
and walkers, being the longest route
between the two extremities of the UK
mainland, measuring 838 miles by the
shortest distance. The fastest time by a
conventional two-wheel bike was set in
2001 by Gethin Butler and took him just
over 44 hours, although most cyclists
take between ten and fourteen days
travelling on quiet roads. US Pilot Rick
Ryan completed the route in a wheelchair
in eight and a half days in 2009.

Failure is our best teacher

Says Richard Holloway, and adds,
'Sadly, there is something about public
life that seems to make it difficult for
people to be honest about
their mistakes.'

Fax machine

Alexander Bain obtained a patent in 1843 for 'improvements in producing and regulating electric currents and improvements in timepieces and in electric printing and signal telegraphs', aka a fax – 30 years before the telephone was invented!

Fingerprinting

Dr Henry Faulds from Beith published the first paper establishing the uniqueness of everyone's fingerprints in 1880.

Flush toilet

Alexander Cumming, an Edinburgh watchmaker, patented the S-trap toilet in 1775, keeping those nasty smells away and it's still in use today – in Scotland at least!

Football internationals

The first ever soccer international took place between Scotland and England in Partick in 1872, following a public challenge issued in Glasgow and Edinburgh newspapers, and ended 0–0. This fixture became a regular event with crowds close to 150,000 turning out regularly at Hampden Park after it was built in 1903.

Freshwater pearl mussel

Living in clean, sandy and gravelly riverbeds, pearl mussels make them even cleaner by filtering up to 30 litres of water a day, contributing to the growth of young trout and salmon.

Glasgow School of Art

Founded in 1845, the school has produced most of Scotland's leading contemporary artists including, since 2005, 30 per cent of Turner Prize nominees and three recent winners: Simon Starling in 2005, Richard Wright in 2009 and Martin Boyce in 2011.

Glasgow's 'Statue of Liberty'

James Alexander Ewing, when redesigning the exterior sculpture of Glasgow City Chambers in 1886 to commemorate Queen Victoria's Golden Jubilee, paid tribute to the iconic Statue of Liberty in New York by modelling his figure of 'Truth' on its American counterpart.

Glasgow Subway Challenge

Getting off at Buchanan Street
and racing the Clockwork Orange
(Underground) downhill to board the
same train at St Enoch. Do you have to
buy another ticket?

The God Particle

Professor Peter Higgs, emeritus
Professor of Edinburgh University,
first hypothesised the existence of the
elusive particle, or boson, thought to be
the means by which everything in the
Universe obtains its mass. Hence the
well-known (though possibly not quite so
well understood) Higgs Boson. This idea
came to him in a moment of inspiration
while walking in the Cairngorms in 1964.

Grand Theft Auto

One of the leading action-adventure
video games in the world, first launched
in 1997 and developed by DMA Design
whose four originators hail from Dundee.

Patrick Grant

Fought against the English in the 1745 Uprising supporting Bonnie Prince Charlie. Grant was subsequently introduced to George IV as 'His Majesty's Oldest Enemy' on a royal visit to Edinburgh nearly 80 years later in 1822. The King offered Grant and his daughter a state pension, and there is a portrait of Grant, painted in the same year, hanging in the Scottish National Portrait Gallery. He died in 1824.

The Great Kilt

Evolved over the course of the sixteenth century from the previous brat, cloak or plaid which was worn over a tunic. With the increasing availability of wool, the kilt grew in size up to 1500 mm wide and 4200 mm long, and was worn day and night both as a cloak and a sleeping blanket, to keep out the elements.

Haggis

A fabulous Scottish signature dish, not just for Burns Night – and perhaps not originally from Scotland. The first known recorded recipe is from Lancashire in 1430!

Hallowe'en
(or All Hallows Eve)

Scottish variant of the evening before All Hallows or All Souls day, first described as such in the sixteenth century. Similar to other Day of the Dead celebrations around the world, it incorporates pagan and Celtic elements.

Hampden Park

Archibald Leitch was the architect responsible for the design of this celebrated football ground. Born in Glasgow in 1865, Archie went on to design Celtic Park, Ibrox, Tynecastle, Anfield, White Hart Lane, Arsenal Stadium and Old Trafford grounds.

Harray Potter

The name coined by that illustrious
Orcadian bookseller Tam McPhail
for Andrew Appleby, master potter at
Fursbreck Pottery in Harray, Orkney.

Heart of Midlothian

A heart-shaped mosaic pattern built into the roadway close to St Giles' Cathedral in central Edinburgh, marking the site of the Old Tolbooth which was both a prison and site of execution until its demolition in 1817. People can often still be seen spitting on this heart: although this action is now thought simply to bring good luck, it was originally intended to show popular disdain for the prison and its notorious activities.

The historical novel

Development of this continuingly popular
form is generally attributed to the
very prolific and popular Walter Scott.
His Waverley novels were incredibly
successful in the nineteenth century
and gave their collective name to
Edinburgh's Waverley Station. When
he died in his Abbotsford palatial home
near Melrose in the Scottish Borders, his
funeral procession was over a mile long.

Hollow pipe drainage

Sir Hugh Dalrymple from Edinburgh invented hollow-pipe drainage in the middle of the eighteenth century. This helped bring large areas of water-logged ground under agricultural production. Subsequently more popularly known as a French Drain, not as another expression of the Auld Alliance, but after Henry French, an American lawyer and government official.

Sherlock Holmes

The fictional detective was created by Arthur Conan Doyle, who found inspiration in a Dr Joseph Bell at the Edinburgh Royal Infirmary for whom he had worked as a clerk. The first novel, *A Study in Scarlet*, was published in 1887.

Hypnotism

James Braid of Kinross coined the modern concept and practice of 'hypnotism' in 1841 and described it as 'a state of physical relaxation accompanied and induced by mental concentration'.

Hypodermic syringe

Another expression of the Auld Alliance: both Alexander Wood, a physician from Cupar, and Charles Pravaz, a French orthopaedic surgeon, invented this independently of each other in 1853.

Infant schools

The very first infant school in the UK was opened in 1816 by Robert Owen in New Lanark as part of his social experimentation and philosophy.

Elsie Inglis

Established a maternity hospital in Edinburgh for poor women and the Scottish Federation of Women's Suffrage Societies, and was active in sending teams of women to help nurse the injured in the First World War in France, Russia and Serbia.

Insulin

John James Rickard Macleod was awarded the Nobel Prize for Physiology or Medicine in 1923 for his part in the discovery of insulin.

Irn-Bru

Now manufactured in Cumbernauld and available worldwide, especially in parts of the globe where there is a significant number of Scots! The distinctively flavoured and coloured fizzy drink is thought to be associated with the re-building of Glasgow's Central Station and its steel supplier at the beginning of the twentieth century. Originally known as Strachan's Brew, the name was changed to Irn-Bru in 1946 to comply with legislation that prohibited the term 'brew' for liquids that were not in fact brewed.

Is compassion really at the heart of religion?

Asked Richard Holloway, former Bishop of Edinburgh in the Scottish Episcopal Church, in a newspaper article in 2010.

Jam Tarts

The affectionate nickname for Edinburgh football club 'Heart of Midlothian' founded in 1874 – also known as Hearts. The name was taken from the infamous site of the Old Tolbooth Jail and Execution site in Edinburgh's High Street.

Jeely piece

The name for jam and bread as a children's snack – and made even more famous by a song written in the 1960s that described the problem of throwing snacks out of the windows of the new high-rise Castlemilk Flats to children twenty storeys below. There were many problems in the low-rise inner city slums they were relocated from but getting hold of your piece wasn't one of them!

Sophia Jex-Blake

Was one of the very first women ever to be enrolled for medical training by Edinburgh University. Despite passing with flying colours, she was prevented from working in hospital wards and hence couldn't graduate in Scotland. She obtained her licence to practice in Dublin, then returned to Scotland and established the Edinburgh School of Medicine for Women in 1886.

Johnnie Walker

Is the name of one of the most successful blended whiskies in the world. It originated in a Kilmarnock grocery shop owned by one John 'Johnnie' Walker – although it was his son and his grandson, both called Alexander Walker, who developed the business under the brand Walker's Kilmarnock Whiskies.

Jute, Jam and Journalism

Established the worldwide reputation
of Dundee.

Kaleidoscope

David Brewster from Jedburgh invented this amazing device in 1815. The kaleidoscope became very popular throughout the UK, in France and the USA, and such was his celebrity status that the inventor's portrait appeared on the inside of cigar boxes.

King James Bible

Celebrated the 400th anniversary of its publication in 2011. King James VI had been on the Scottish throne since 1567, and shortly after the merger of the crowns in 1603 authorised a new English translation of both the Old and New Testaments which he hoped would settle various religious disputes and stand the test of time. It was published in 1611 and sold for ten shillings.

The Labour Party

Kier Hardie, born in North Lanarkshire, became an MP in 1892 and helped set up the modern-day Labour Party. He wore a cloth cap to Parliament, believed in a progressive income tax, universal suffrage, free pensions for the elderly and the abolition of the House of Lords. A man ahead of his time!

Lady the osprey

Lady, one of the oldest ospreys in the world, returned to Loch of the Lowes Wildlife Reserve near Dunkeld in 2011 for her twenty-first annual visit. She has laid sixty-one eggs and seen forty-eight chicks leave her nest, which is now the size of a double bed. She spends her winters in the Gambia.

Langoustine
(*Nephrops norvegicus*)

Over one third of all world landings of this most valuable and delicious seafood is brought ashore in Scotland. In 2009, 31,490 tonnes were landed at a value of over £78 million.

Lawnmower

Alexander Shanks from Arbroath is
credited with creating the first 'horse-
drawn grass cutting machine', which
was trialled in 1842. Why not visit the
Arbroath Lawnmower Collection?

Lewis Chessmen

Unearthed in Uig Bay on the Isle of Lewis in 1831, but originating in Norway, most of these pieces are carved from walrus ivory, with the others being made from whales' teeth. Thought to be one of the few remaining complete medieval chess sets, only eleven of the seventy-eight pieces are exhibited in Scotland – with the remainder on display in London!

Lime cordial

Lauchlan Rose patented Rose's Lime Juice in 1867, and it went into production in Leith the following year. Simultaneously, the British Navy required all sailors to be issued with a lime ration to prevent scurvy, and its use became so ubiquitous that British sailors became known as 'limeys'.

Little Sparta

Ian Hamilton Finlay embraced and extended the concept of concrete poetry, a concept coined in the 1950s, not only in his writing as a poet but also as an artist and a gardener. The poem as object can be seen expressed in the form of stone, metal and wood in the five-acre 'Little Sparta' garden situated in the Pentland Hills just south of Edinburgh. It has been described by Roy Strong as 'the only really original garden made in this country since 1945'.

Local Hero

The enduringly popular film *Local Hero* made in 1983 by Bill Forsyth has made Pennan and its notable red telephone box world famous. Pennan, where the film was shot, is actually situated on the East coast between Macduff and Fraserburgh, but purports to be the fictitious west-coast village Furness on the screen.

Loch Morar

The deepest freshwater loch in Scotland – and the deepest lake in Europe at 310 metres. Great wild fishing, and one of the few large lochs in the country to be unaffected by the influences of fish farming.

Loch Ness

At more than 750 feet (228 m) the waters of Loch Ness are deeper than the North Sea. The *Journal of Geophysical Research* has recently reported that the loch tilts back and forth with the passing of the tides by 1.5 mm, like a giant spirit level.

Logarithms and Napier's Bones

Both of these ingenious mathematical methods (Napier's Bones is a type of abacus) were invented by John Napier of Edinburgh in the early seventeenth century. He died of gout.

'The Lord is My Shepherd' in Scots (extract)

The Lord is my Shepherd
in nocht am I wantin'
In the haugh's green girse
does He mak me lie doon
While mony puir straiglers
are bleatin' and pantin'
By saft-flowin' burnies
He leads me at noon.

Macadam road construction

John Loudon McAdam introduced road surfaces constructed from single-sized aggregate layers of stone with a coating of binder as a cementing agent in around 1820.

Giant Angus MacAskill

Born in Berneray in the Western Isles, Angus and his family emigrated to Nova Scotia as a result of the Highland Clearances when he was six years old in 1831. Although he was a smaller than average baby, he grew to an enormous 7 ft 9 in. tall, and is still thought to be both the tallest and strongest man in history, being recorded as lifting a 1,300 kg anchor. There is a museum dedicated to him in Dunvegan, Skye.

Lady Macbeth

This fictional character is often seen as a metaphor for the conflict between masculinity and femininity – which has been evident in all societies and all cultures everywhere throughout history. Does she suppress her instincts toward compassion, motherhood and fragility in favour of ambition, ruthlessness and the single-minded pursuit of power?

Maggie's Centres

The Maggie's Cancer Caring Centres Trust was founded by Maggie Keswick Jencks in 1995 to provide support for people affected by cancer, their families, carers and friends. It aims to empower people to live with, through and beyond cancer. The first Maggie's Centre opened in Edinburgh in 1996.

A man that dies rich, dies disgraced

So wrote Dunfermline-born industrialist
and social reformer Andrew Carnegie
in 1889.

Modern steam engine

Greenock-born James Watt, repairing an engine in 1763 while working at Glasgow University, realised that he could make it far more efficient by adding a separate condenser, thus requiring less fuel and generating more power. He received a patent for the modern steam engine in 1769. He also developed the concept of horsepower, and the electrical measurement, the watt, was named after him.

James Murdoch

Journalist and genius in foreign languages, this historical James Murdoch was born in Stonehaven in 1856. He resigned his post as professor and emigrated to Australia at the age of twenty-four. He is celebrated for his three-volume *History of Japan*.

'My Old Man's a Dustman'

This song was written by Lonnie Donegan, known as the King of Skiffle, who was born in Glasgow. The song made No. 1 in the hit parade in 1960.

Neurosis

Coined by the Scottish doctor William Cullen in 1769 to refer to 'disorders of sense and motion' caused by a 'general affection of the nervous system'.

The New York Herald

Established by James Gordon Bennett Senior in 1835. Born in Banffshire, he entered a Roman Catholic seminary, then emigrated to America where he became a teacher, then a journalist and subsequently a newspaper proprietor. Over the next thirty years it enjoyed the highest circulation in the US of any newspaper.

The noble gases

Comprising neon, xenon, helium, krypton, argon and radon, they were all discovered by the celebrated Nobel Prize-winning Glaswegian chemist William Ramsay at the end of the nineteenth century. He is also associated with a less successful project to extract gold from seawater.

Northern Lighthouse Board

Established originally in 1786, the Board now controls 212 lighthouses, 154 buoys and 47 beacons remotely from its headquarters in Edinburgh's George Street. Sadly there are no longer any resident lighthouse keepers.

Old Crow
Bourbon Whiskey

Established by Edinburgh emigrant,
chemist and distiller James Crow in
Kentucky in the 1830s.

Over the sea to Skye

From 'The Skye Boat Song', there are now two routes along which to sing this: driving along the 'Road to the Isles' to catch the CalMac ferry from Mallaig – or whilst crossing the toll-free Skye Bridge from Kyle of Lochalsh.

Paper money

John Law, from Cramond, was known
as a philanderer, gambler and duellist,
but is also credited with the invention of
the folding stuff at the beginning of the
eighteenth century.

Paraffin

James Young was born in Glasgow in 1811 and successfully extracted a number of useful liquids by distillation at a low heat from types of coal found close by his factory in Bathgate. One of these could be stored both in liquid and solid form, and this he called paraffin. He established patents successfully in the UK and US, and was affectionately known as 'Paraffin' Young.

Peter Pan

Originally written as a play by J. M. Barrie from Kirriemuir in 1904, it was later turned into a book and, in 1953, into a Disney cartoon film.

The Physiognomy of Mental Diseases

Written by Sir Alexander Morison and published in 1840, this treatise was based on the hypothesis that a patient's, indeed anyone's, facial expression revealed their underlying mental condition. There is a remarkable portrait of Morison hanging in the Scottish National Portrait Gallery, painted by Richard Dadd in 1852, in which the subject appears weary and somewhat miserable. Dadd was a celebrated Victorian painter, and a patient of Morison's, but he sadly spent most of his adult life in the 'mental' institutions of Bethlem and Broadmoor.

Pinkerton Detective Agency

Established by Gorbals-born Allan Pinkerton in 1850 in Chicago. Its motto was 'We Never Sleep' and in their early years the detectives were famous for solving a series of train robberies and failing to catch Jesse James.

The Poker Club

A thinking and drinking club set up in Edinburgh early in the second half of the eighteenth century. Key characters involved in the Scottish Enlightenment met regularly in an atmosphere of 'convivial sociability' to share ideas and to promote the argument for a Scottish militia. The poker in the title refers to 'stirring things up', rather than card playing.

Queensberry Rules

John Sholto Douglas, 9th Marquess of Queensberry, sponsored and endorsed the creation of a code of rules that was published in 1867 and which laid down the modern basis for boxing. The rules took his name but were written, in fact, by John Graham Chambers.

Radar defence system

Robert Watson-Watt, from Brechin, having proved scientifically that Nazi Germany could not possibly possess a death ray using radio waves (something much rumoured and feared in the late 1930s), subsequently went on to establish the first effective radar defence network based both on land and in the air. This eventually made a significant contribution to the successful ending of the Battle of Britain.

The Railplane

George Bennie constructed a novel form of monorail system in a railway siding in Milngavie in the 1920s. Powered by fore and aft aircraft propellers, the Railplane was launched in 1930 to great general enthusiasm and there was even a proposal to build a route between Edinburgh and Glasgow. Unable to find sufficient backing however, he was declared bankrupt in 1937 and by 1960 all was demolished or sold for scrap. See the film at Glasgow Transport Museum.

Refrigeration

William Cullen, yet another central figure of the Scottish Enlightenment, was a chemist, physician and agriculturalist. In 1756 he gave the first documented demonstration of artificial refrigeration – but the process was considered to have no commercial application at the time.

Rest and be Thankful

These are the words inscribed on a stone near the viewpoint on the A83 as it goes through the Arrochar Alps. The words were placed there by soldiers who built the original military road in 1753.

Robinson Crusoe

This famous novel, written by Daniel Defoe and published in 1719, is almost certainly inspired by the true-life experiences of Alexander Selkirk who was born in Lower Largo on the Fife Coast forty years previously. Running away to sea, Selkirk was subsequently marooned for over four years on one of the Juan Fernández Islands off the west coast of Chile. After being rescued and returning to the UK, Selkirk's solitary life on the island and the serenity and calmness that he displayed were much discussed.

RRS *Discovery*

Now berthed in her home town Dundee
as a popular visitor attraction, this
was the last traditional wooden three-
masted ship to be built in Britain. Her
first mission was the British National
Antarctic Expedition carrying Robert
Falcon Scott and Ernest Shackleton,
which set sail from the Isle of Wight in
August 1901. Despite being locked in
ice for two years, the expedition was
a success and established that the
Antarctic was indeed a continent.

St Trinian's

While training as a Sapper in Kirkcudbright at the beginning of the Second World War, the recently deceased cartoonist Ronald Searle was taken in by a local couple whose two daughters had been evacuated from their school, St Trinnean's in Edinburgh. Searle started sketching there and sent a cartoon to Kaye Webb, an editor at *Lilliput* magazine, in which a group of girls with hockey sticks were reading a notice that said, 'Owing to the international situation, the match with St Trinian's has been postponed'. The cartoon was subsequently published and after the war Searle and Webb were married.

Saki

The nom de plume of Hector Hugh
Munro, son of Scotsman Charles
Augustus Munro, Saki became a
celebrated journalist and satirist in
Edwardian times. Not to be confused
with sake, the Japanese rice-based
alcoholic drink, or the White-faced Saki,
a South American monkey.

Scotch

Is only drunk outside Scotland. Here, a great deal of whisky is consumed.

Scotch Argus butterfly

Loves damp, lush, open grassland and full sun in the north and west of Scotland – with hundreds to be found in Glen Douglas.

Scotch pies

The original fast food; of variable
quality and often eaten at half-time
(at football matches).

Scottish beer

Brewing in Scotland goes back over 5,000 years – it has been suggested that beer may have been brewed from barley at Skara Brae, the Neolithic site in Orkney.

Scottish crannogs

Artificial or modified natural islands found in many Scottish lochs. Built as defensive homesteads from as early as 5,000 years ago and in some cases used until the seventeenth century, their heyday was during the Bronze Age from *c.*750 BC to *c.*42 AD. The Scottish Crannog Centre on Loch Tay is a re-creation built on stilts based on the design of an underwater excavation from 2,600 years ago. Oddly, midges do not seem to bite in the Crannog which is away from the water's edge.

The Scottish Enlightenment

This philosophical movement took place between 1730 and 1800 when Scotland was at the intellectual forefront of the western world. Its participant thinkers aimed to construct first principles of politics and society free from the religious underpinning that had previously dominated thinking. The movement encompassed philosophy, chemistry, geology, architecture, poetry, engineering, technology, economics, sociology, medicine and history.

Scottish Parliament Building, Holyrood, Edinburgh

Designed by the Spanish architect Enric Miralles, the building was built on the former Scottish & Newcastle brewery site and opened in 2004 to both criticism and acclaim. It went on to win numerous awards and has been described by Charles Jencks as 'a tour de force of arts and crafts and quality without parallel in the last 100 years of British architecture'.

Sea eagle

These rare and massive birds (an eight foot wingspan) became extinct throughout the UK but were re-introduced to Scotland on the Island of Rum in 1975. There are now over fifty breeding pairs, which can be seen at various locations along the west coast.

Selkirk Bannock

The most famous of all bannocks; said to have been first made by Robbie Douglas in Selkirk in 1859, and immortalised by Queen Victoria's eating a piece when she visited Abbotsford, Walter Scott's house nearby. Made from wheat flour, butter and a great number of sultanas. Delicious!

Short-tailed Iron Age sheep

Known as the Dunface, this breed survived in the Scottish Highlands until around 1880, although there are still some descendants in a few remote islands.

The Skating Minister

The image of Reverend Robert Walker skating on Duddingston Loch has in recent decades become a celebrated icon of Scottish culture, having been painted by Henry Raeburn at the height of the Scottish Enlightenment. It is exhibited in the National Gallery of Scotland in Edinburgh.

Sociology

The 'father of modern sociology' was Adam Ferguson, also known as Ferguson of Raith, yet another leading figure of the Scottish Enlightenment. He may well have fought under the Duke of Cumberland (!) at the Battle of Fontenoy during the War of Austrian Succession in 1745 before developing his academic and philosophic studies.

Spurtle

A uniquely shaped wooden stick for stirring porridge. There is a World Porridge-Making Championship held every year in Carrbridge with the winner claiming the 'Golden Spurtle'.

Steam hammer

James Naysmyth from Edinburgh invented this in around 1837. From its outset Naysmyth was keen to show its versatility: it could crack an egg resting in a wineglass without breaking the glass and then with the next blow, shake the whole building.

Stereotyping

Originally invented by William Ged in 1725, this is a process that revolutionised printing. It involved creating a plaster mould of the original type and then casting it in metal. The result was also known as the stereotype or cliché, a term that came to mean a well-known and over-used expression to describe situations and people.

The Stone of Destiny

Also known as The Stone of Scone, it weighs 152 kg and is now safely back in Scotland. It was used for centuries for the coronation of Scottish monarchs, but stolen by Longshanks, the English sovereign otherwise known as Edward I in 1296. It was attacked by the Suffragettes in 1914 and whisked away from Westminster by four Scottish students in 1950.

Sulphuric acid

The lead chamber process for its
distillation was invented by John
Roebuck of Prestonpans in 1746.

Tactical Nuclear Penguin

Claims to be the 'world's strongest' beer at 32 per cent proof. Made by BrewDog in Fraserburgh, who advise that it should be drunk discerningly 'in exactly the same manner that you would enjoy a fine whisky or a Frank Zappa album.'

The telegraph

An anonymous writer in *The Scots Magazine* of 1753 suggested the principles of an electrostatic telegraph, using an individual wire for each letter of the alphabet. It was considered to be impractical at the time.

Teleprinter

Prototype built by Frederick G. Creed
in 1912 from an old typewriter that he
bought in Sauchiehall Street Market.
Watch those old football results
clickety-clack.

Thermos flask

More properly known as a vacuum flask, this was invented by Scottish physicist and chemist Sir James Dewar in 1892. He failed to register a patent, and it was subsequently patented by a German company – Thermos GmbH.

Thomas the Rhymer

This thirteenth-century laird came from Earlston and wrote many prophetic verses on Scottish history, temptation and mortal pleasures. He is most famous for his encounter with the Queen of Faeries. There is a memorial to him (at the legendary location of this notable episode) overlooking the Tweed and the new Melrose crematorium.

Titan Crane

Built in 1907, the Clydebank Titan Crane helped establish the worldwide reputation of John Brown Shipbuilders. The cantilever design was revolutionary at the time and the arm of the crane measures 240 feet in length. It weighs 800 tons and is 150 foot high, and has been modified to lift 200 tons. The Clydebank Titan was converted into a visitor attraction for its centenary in 2007. Brave folk can journey up in a lift and stand on the jib – and abseil down (by arrangement only).

Tree guards

A type of tubular plastic shelter (sometimes described as a vertical greenhouse) used to nurture trees in the early stages of their growth, keeping out herbivores, chemicals and the worst of the climate! Created in 1979 by Graham Tuley, the tree guard was considered to be one of the hundred best inventions in the first International Inventors Awards in 1986.

Ultimo Bras

Founded by Michelle Mone from Glasgow. Its launch, held at Selfridges in London in August 1999, became the most successful bra event in the UK with six weeks' worth of stock sold in less than 24 hours.

Ultrasound

Ian Donald from the University of Glasgow published a paper in *The Lancet* in 1958, outlining the medical uses of ultrasound after having seen it used in the shipyards to identify flaws in metallurgy.

Universal Standard Time

Sir Sandford Fleming was born in Kirkcaldy and in 1845 emigrated to Canada, where he achieved fame as an engineer and inventor. He was responsible for much of the Canada Pacific Railway and proposed a system of twenty-four international standard time zones after missing a train in Ireland. Although rejected in his lifetime, all major countries had adopted the system by 1929.

Up Helly Aa

The largest Fire Festival in Europe takes place in various locations in Shetland every year on the last Tuesday in January and marks the end of the Yule season. It involves large processions of people holding torches that are ultimately thrown to ignite a replica Viking longship. Performances, dancing, music, feasting and drinking abound.

Utopian Socialism

Influenced Robert Owen in his development of the model community at New Lanark in the first quarter of the nineteenth century. He implemented revolutionary ideas in the fields of childcare, education, healthcare, co-operatives and the trade union movement.

'Waltzing Matilda'

Written in 1895 by Andrew Barton 'Banjo' Paterson, the son of a Lanarkshire emigrant to Australia, it is said to be based on a melody written by fellow Scot, James Barr, entitled 'Go to the Devil and Shake Yourself'. 'Waltzing Matilda', however, is not the Australian national anthem (as commonly but erroneously thought).

The Wealth of Nations

First published in 1776, at the very
beginning of the Industrial Revolution,
Adam Smith's ground-breaking work
laid out the definitive arguments
for free market capitalism. Born in
Kirkcaldy, he now rests in Canongate
Kirkyard alongside one of his relatives
Ebenezer Lennox Scroggie, who was
the inspiration for Dickens' character
Ebenezer Scrooge.

West Highland Line

Considered to be one of the most scenic railway journeys in the world, running between Fort William and Mallaig. Summer trains are often pulled by steam engines and traverse the Glenfinnan Viaduct (famous for its appearance in the Harry Potter films), and of course pass the spot where Bonnie Prince Charlie landed in 1745, arriving from France via Eriskay.

Whisky Mac

Another drink made from Scottish
ingredients but named elsewhere.
Whisky is obviously the critical element,
but so too is ginger wine, much of which
was made by Crabbies in their Leith
distillery from 1801 until 1990.

... and of course there is always...

One o'clock gun • Clyde puffers • Arbroath Smokie • Pneumatic tyres • Scottish oatcakes • Border Reivers • Midges • Robert the Bruce's spider • 'Flower of Scotland' • Concrete Bob • St Kilda • St Mungo • The Kelvin scale • Shinty • The bonnie, bonnie banks of Loch Lomond • Cullen Skink • Stac Polly • St Andrew's Day • Samye Ling Monastery • Burns suppers • Granite City • Caledonian Pine Forest • Free prescriptions • The East Neuk • Smoo Cave

... and not forgetting...

£4.99
Hardback
ISBN: 978-0-95536-411-2

**WHIT'S FUR YE'LL NO
GO BY YE!**
**Timeless Scottish wisdom
for every occasion**

£4.99
Hardback
ISBN: 978-1-908661-00-5

**... and Other Great Things
from Scotland**

www.bookspeed.com/doodle

BRAW
STUFF
FAE
SCOTLAND

BRAW
STUFF
FAE
SCOTLAND

BR
STU
FA
SCOTL

RAW
UFF
E
AND

BRAW
STUFF
FAE
SCOTLAND

BRAW
STUFF
FAE
SCOTLAND

BRAW
STUFF
FAE
SCOTLAND

BRAW
STUFF
FAE
SCOTLAND

BR
STU
FA
SCOTL

AW
UFF
E
AND

BRAW
STUFF
FAE
SCOTLAND

BRAW
STUFF
FAE
SCOTLAND

BRAW STUFF FAE SCOTLAND

BRAW STUFF FAE SCOTLAND
BRAW STUFF FAE SCOTLAND
BRAW STUFF FAE SCOTLAND
BRAW STUFF FAE SCOTLAND
BRAW STUFF FAE SCOTLAND